YOUR COMPLETE CANCER 2024 PERSONAL HOROSCOPE

Monthly Astrological Prediction Forecast Readings of Every Zodiac Astrology Sun Star Signs- Love, Romance, Money, Finances, Career, Health, Travel, Spirituality.

Iris Quinn

Alpha Zuriel Publishing

Your Complete Cancer 2024 Personal Horoscope/ Iris Quinn. - - 1st ed.

"In the dance of the planets, we find the rhythms of life. Astrology reminds us that we are all connected to the greater universe, and our actions have ripple effects throughout the cosmos."
— IRIS QUINN

CONTENTS

CHAPTER ONE

CANCER PROFILE

- Constellation: Cancer
- Zodiac Symbol: The Crab
- Date: June 21 - July 22
- Element: Water
- Ruling Planet: Moon
- Career Planet: Mercury
- Love Planet: Venus
- Money Planet: Moon
- Planet of Fun, Entertainment, Creativity, and Speculations: Neptune
- Planet of Health and Work: Saturn
- Planet of Home and Family Life: Moon
- Planet of Spirituality: Pluto
- Planet of Travel, Education, Religion, and Philosophy: Jupiter

Colors:

- Colors: Silver, Sea Green
- Colors that promote love, romance, and social harmony: Pale Blue, Pearl White
- Color that promotes earning power: Silver

Gem: Moonstone

- Metals: Silver, Platinum
- Scent: Sea Breeze
- Birthstone: Ruby

Cancer Qualities:

- Quality: Cardinal (Initiating)
- Quality most needed for balance: Assertiveness

Cancer Virtues:

- Nurturing Nature
- Emotional Sensitivity
- Intuition
- Empathy
- Protective Instincts

Deepest Need: Emotional Security

Characteristics to Embrace:

- Compassion
- Creativity

- Loyalty
- Adaptability

Signs of Greatest Overall Compatibility:
- Scorpio
- Pisces

Signs of Greatest Overall Incompatibility:
- Aries
- Libra
- Capricorn

- Sign Most Supportive for Career Advancement: Capricorn
- Sign Most Supportive for Emotional Well-being: Cancer
- Sign Most Supportive Financially: Taurus
- Sign Best for Marriage and/or Partnerships: Scorpio
- Sign Most Supportive for Creative Projects: Pisces
- Best Sign to Have Fun With: Leo

Signs Most Supportive in Spiritual Matters:
- Sagittarius
- Pisces

Best Day of the Week: Monday

CANCER TRAITS

- Sensitive and empathetic.
- Nurturing and caring.
- Intuitive and guided by instincts.
- Protective of loved ones.
- Deep attachment to home and family.
- Imaginative and creative.
- Loyal and committed.
- Prone to mood swings.
- Tenacious and determined.
- Empathetic and understanding.

PERSONALITY OF CANCER

In the depths of the zodiac lies the enchanting and empathetic soul of Cancer. Like the ebb and flow of the tides, they are intimately connected to their emotions, allowing their intuition to guide them through the intricate tapestry of life.

With a heart that beats to the rhythm of love, Cancer individuals are the eternal caregivers of the zodiac. They possess a nurturing spirit, like a warm embrace that soothes weary souls and offers solace in times of need. Their compassion knows no bounds, as they navigate the labyrinth of emotions with grace and understanding.

Home is their sanctuary, a haven of love and security. Cancer individuals create a tapestry of memories within the walls, infusing every nook and cranny with their tender touch. They find joy in tending to their nest, nurturing their loved ones with delicious meals, gentle embraces, and a listening ear that understands the unspoken.

In the depths of their imagination, Cancer
individuals find solace. They are the dreamers, the
poets, and the artists who paint the world with hues of
emotion. Their creativity flows like a river, carrying
them to distant shores of inspiration, where they
capture the essence of life in brushstrokes and
melodies.

Loyalty is their silent anthem, echoing through the
chambers of their soul. Once they forge a connection,
it becomes an unbreakable bond, woven with threads
of trust and unwavering devotion. They are the
warriors who stand guard, shielding their loved ones
from the stormy winds that life may bring.

Yet, like the moon, their emotions wax and wane,
casting shadows upon their path. Their sensitivity can
be both their strength and their vulnerability, as they
navigate the ever-changing currents of their own heart.
They seek moments of solitude, to retreat into the
gentle whispers of their emotions, finding solace in the
sanctuary of self-reflection.

But within the depths of their watery essence lies a
tenacity that cannot be extinguished. Cancer
individuals possess a fierce determination, fueled by
their emotional connection to their dreams. They
navigate the rocky terrain of life with unwavering

resolve, their spirit shining brightly even in the darkest of times.

In the embrace of Cancer's tender heart, you will find a compassionate soul who holds your dreams with delicate hands and stands by your side through the tides of life. They are the moonlit guides, illuminating the path with their intuitive wisdom and reminding us all of the power of love, empathy, and emotional depth.

WEAKNESSES OF CANCER

In the gentle depths of a Cancer's soul, vulnerabilities whisper like delicate melodies. Their sensitive nature, like fragile petals, can be both their strength and their weakness, for their emotions ebb and flow like the tides, sometimes overwhelming their fragile shores.

Wrapped in the loving embrace of empathy, Cancer individuals can become entangled in the web of their own emotions. Like a sailor lost at sea, they may find themselves navigating treacherous waters, their hearts vulnerable to the storms that rage within. Their deep connection to their own feelings can at times leave them feeling adrift, longing for the stability of solid ground.

With their tender hearts exposed, Cancer individuals may retreat into the safety of their shells, seeking refuge from the harsh realities of the world. Their fear of rejection and being hurt can create barriers, shielding them from fully expressing their emotions and vulnerability. In their quest to protect their hearts, they may inadvertently build walls that hinder their growth and inhibit intimate connections.

The moon, their celestial guide, influences their moods like the shifting tides. Cancer individuals can be prone to mood swings, riding the waves of emotions with intensity and unpredictability. Their loved ones may struggle to understand the ever-changing landscape of their feelings, as they navigate the currents of joy, sadness, and everything in between.

Like a crab retreating into its shell, Cancer individuals can be cautious and hesitant when faced with unfamiliar territory. Their fear of stepping outside their comfort zone may limit their growth and prevent them from fully embracing new experiences. They may find themselves trapped in the safety of familiarity, missing out on the transformative magic that lies beyond their protective walls.

Cancer's deep sense of attachment can sometimes lead to clinginess and possessiveness. Their desire for emotional security and closeness may cause them to hold tightly to those they cherish, fearing the pain of separation. This intense need for connection can place strains on relationships, as their loved ones may yearn for freedom and independence.

Yet, within the vulnerabilities lie the seeds of resilience. Cancer individuals have the power to transform their weaknesses into strengths, to learn to navigate the tides of their emotions with grace and balance. By embracing their sensitivity, cultivating healthy boundaries, and finding the courage to step beyond their shells, they can harness the power of their emotional depth and create a world where vulnerability becomes their greatest source of strength.

RELATIONSHIP COMPATIBILITY WITH CANCER

Based only on their Sun signs, this is how Cancer interacts with others. These are the compatibility interpretations for all 12 potential Cancer combinations. This is a limited and insufficient method of determining compatibility.

However, Sun-sign compatibility remains the foundation for overall harmony in a relationship.

The general rule is that yin and yang do not get along. Yin complements yin, and yang complements yang. While yin and yang partnerships can be successful, they require more effort. Earth and water zodiac signs are both Yin. Yang is represented by the fire and air zodiac signs.

Cancer (Yin) and Aries (Yang)

When Cancer and Aries come together, they bring together the energies of sensitivity and assertiveness. Cancer's nurturing nature complements Aries' boldness, creating a dynamic and passionate bond. However, conflicts may arise due to their different approaches to emotions and decision-making. Cancer's need for security and emotional connection may clash with Aries' desire for independence. With open communication and mutual respect, they can navigate these differences and create a relationship filled with emotional depth, support, and excitement.

Cancer (Yin) and Taurus (Yin)

The union of two Cancer individuals is marked by deep emotional connection and shared values. They understand each other's needs for security, loyalty, and nurturing, creating a loving and stable partnership. Their mutual devotion to creating a warm and harmonious home environment strengthens their bond. However, both Cancer partners need to be mindful of getting too caught up in their emotions, as it may lead to moodiness or over-dependence. By cultivating healthy boundaries and open communication, they can build a lasting and fulfilling relationship based on trust and emotional intimacy.

Cancer (Yin) and Gemini (Yang)

The pairing of Cancer and Gemini brings together emotional depth and intellectual curiosity. Cancer's sensitivity and nurturing nature complement Gemini's wit and adaptability. However, their different approaches to emotions may pose challenges in their relationship. Cancer seeks emotional security and connection, while Gemini values mental stimulation and variety. Both partners need to find a balance between emotional expression and intellectual engagement. With patience, understanding, and a willingness to learn from each other, they can create a relationship that combines emotional depth, intellectual growth, and shared adventures.

Cancer (Yin) and Cancer (Yin)

When two Cancer individuals come together, their shared Yin energy creates a deeply nurturing and emotionally connected bond. They understand each other's emotional needs and intuitively provide the support and care they both desire. Their home becomes a sanctuary of love and comfort, where they can openly express their feelings and create lasting memories. However, conflicts may arise due to their sensitive and moody nature. Both partners need to practice open communication and empathy, allowing space for each other's emotional fluctuations. By embracing their shared nurturing instincts and creating a harmonious domestic life, they can build a relationship filled with emotional depth, love, and compassion.

Cancer (Yin) and Leo (Yang)

When Cancer and Leo unite, they create a powerful blend of sensitivity and passion. Cancer's nurturing nature resonates with Leo's desire for admiration and love. They bring out the best in each other, with Cancer offering emotional support and Leo adding excitement and creativity to their lives. However, conflicts may arise due to Cancer's need for security and Leo's desire for attention and validation. Both partners need to cultivate open communication and mutual respect, allowing room for both emotional intimacy and individual expression. With a balance of love, loyalty, and shared adventures, they can build a strong and vibrant partnership.

Cancer (Yin) and Virgo (Yang)

The union of Cancer and Virgo combines emotional depth and practicality. Cancer's nurturing nature finds harmony with Virgo's attention to detail and desire for stability. They share a love for creating a comfortable and organized home environment. However, conflicts may arise due to Cancer's emotional sensitivity and Virgo's critical nature. Both partners need to practice patience and understanding, appreciating each other's strengths and offering support in areas of weakness. By embracing each other's differences and working together, they can build a loving and balanced relationship.

Cancer (Yin) and Libra (Yang)

The pairing of Cancer and Libra blends emotional depth with harmonious connection. Cancer's nurturing nature resonates with Libra's desire for balance and harmony. They create a loving and supportive partnership, appreciating each other's need for emotional connection and social engagement. However, conflicts may arise due to Cancer's moodiness and Libra's desire for peace at all costs. Both partners need to find a balance between emotional expression and compromise. By cultivating open communication and mutual respect, they can build a relationship that combines emotional intimacy, shared values, and social harmony.

Cancer (Yin) and Scorpio (Yang)

When Cancer and Scorpio come together, they create a deep and intense bond. Both signs value emotional connection and loyalty, fostering a relationship built on trust and intimacy. Cancer's nurturing nature complements Scorpio's passion and depth, creating a powerful partnership. However, conflicts may arise due to Cancer's moodiness and Scorpio's intensity. Both partners need to navigate their emotional depths with compassion and patience, allowing space for vulnerability and growth. By embracing their shared emotional intensity and supporting each other's needs, they can create a transformative and enduring relationship.

Cancer (Yin) and Sagittarius (Yang)

The union of Cancer and Sagittarius brings together emotional depth and adventurous spirit. Cancer's nurturing nature finds excitement in Sagittarius' love for exploration and freedom. They can inspire each other to grow and expand their horizons. However, conflicts may arise due to Cancer's need for security and Sagittarius' desire for independence. Both partners need to find a balance between emotional stability and personal freedom. By embracing each other's differences and supporting each other's individual journeys, they can create a relationship filled with emotional depth and shared adventures.

Cancer (Yin) and Capricorn (Yang)

When Cancer and Capricorn come together, they blend emotional depth with practicality and ambition. Cancer's nurturing nature finds stability and security in Capricorn's drive for success. They create a strong and enduring partnership, valuing loyalty and building a solid foundation for their future. However, conflicts may arise due to Cancer's sensitivity and Capricorn's focus on work and achievements. Both partners need to cultivate open communication and find a balance between emotional connection and career aspirations. By supporting each other's goals and creating a harmonious home environment, they can build a relationship that combines emotional fulfillment and material stability.

Cancer (Yin) and Aquarius (Yang)

The pairing of Cancer and Aquarius blends emotional depth with intellectual curiosity. Cancer's nurturing nature finds stimulation in Aquarius' innovative thinking and independence. They can learn from each other, broadening their perspectives and embracing new ideas. However, conflicts may arise due to Cancer's need for emotional security and Aquarius' desire for personal freedom. Both partners need to find a balance between emotional intimacy and individual expression. By cultivating open-mindedness and honoring each other's unique qualities, they can build a relationship that combines emotional depth and intellectual growth.

Cancer (Yin) and Pisces (Yang)

When Cancer and Pisces unite, they create a deeply intuitive and compassionate bond. Both signs value emotional connection and are attuned to each other's needs. Cancer's nurturing nature finds harmony in Pisces' dreamy and imaginative world. They can create a safe and supportive haven for each other. However, conflicts may arise due to Cancer's moodiness and Pisces' escapism. Both partners need to navigate their emotional landscapes with empathy and understanding. By embracing their shared sensitivity and fostering a deep emotional connection, they can build a relationship that combines emotional depth, creativity, and unconditional love.

LOVE AND PASSION

In the realm of love and passion, Cancer blossoms like a gentle summer rain, captivating hearts with their deep emotional sensitivity and nurturing nature. They are the eternal romantics, seeking a profound and soulful connection that transcends the boundaries of time.

For a Cancer, love is an ocean of emotions, where they dive fearlessly into the depths of their partner's soul. They possess an innate ability to understand and empathize with their loved ones, offering unwavering support and comfort in times of joy and sorrow. Like the moon, they radiate a calming energy that provides solace and security to their beloved.

Passion runs through the veins of Cancer, ignited by the intensity of their emotions. They yearn to express their desires and share their innermost fantasies with a partner who can truly appreciate the depth of their love. Behind their gentle exterior lies a sensual and enchanting spirit, ready to explore the realms of intimacy with an unyielding fervor.

Cancers are devoted and committed lovers, cherishing the sanctity of a long-term partnership. They value loyalty and trust above all else, seeking a soulmate with whom they can build a foundation of unwavering support and shared dreams. They are the keepers of memories, treasuring each intimate moment and weaving them into a tapestry of love that stands the test of time.

However, their emotional nature can also bring forth vulnerabilities. Cancers may experience moments of insecurity and protectiveness, fearing the pain of heartbreak. They crave reassurance and constant affection, seeking a partner who can navigate the ebb and flow of their ever-changing emotions.

When a Cancer falls in love, they offer their heart wholeheartedly, embracing vulnerability as a testament to the depth of their affection. Their love is a tender embrace, a safe haven where their partner can find solace and emotional nourishment.

In the realm of love and passion, Cancer shines as a beacon of tender affection and unyielding devotion. They paint the world with their love, creating a sanctuary of warmth and compassion for their chosen partner. To love a Cancer is to embark on a journey of deep emotional connection, where love knows no bounds and passion is an eternal flame that dances in their soul.

MARRIAGE

Marriage is a sacred bond that holds profound significance for Cancer individuals, as they wholeheartedly embrace the role of a devoted spouse and eagerly embark on the journey of building a family. Both men and women born under this sign approach marriage with a deep sense of commitment and loyalty, valuing the sanctity of their union above all else.

For Cancers, family is the cornerstone of their existence, and they prioritize creating a loving and nurturing home environment for their spouse and children. They take on the role of a protector and provider, offering unwavering affection and support to their loved ones. In times of marital challenges, Cancers display unwavering dedication, going to great lengths to salvage and strengthen their relationship.

Cancers find fulfillment in their roles as housewives or househusbands, relishing in the joys of caring for their children and tending to the needs of their family. They infuse their homes with warmth, creativity, and attention to detail, creating a haven where love and harmony flourish. The comfort and stability they provide are essential pillars of their marital bond.

Male Cancers, in particular, take pride in nurturing their partners and ensuring their emotional well-being. Contrary to societal norms, they embrace their sensitivity and openly express their emotions, making their spouse feel cherished and valued at all times. They strive to create a safe and loving space where their partner can thrive and feel unconditionally loved.

In a marriage with a Cancer, one can expect unwavering loyalty, emotional support, and a deep sense of partnership. They prioritize the well-being and happiness of their spouse, valuing open communication, trust, and mutual respect. Through their commitment and dedication, Cancers seek to create a lifelong union that weathers the storms of life and celebrates the joys of shared love and companionship.

CHAPTER TWO

CANCER 2024 HOROSCOPE

Overview Cancer 2024

Welcome, Cancer, to the year 2024, a year of profound transformation and growth. The celestial bodies have aligned in a way that will bring about significant changes in various aspects of your life. The year will be marked by a series of astrological aspects that will influence your career, relationships, health, and personal development. As the Crab of the Zodiac, you are known for your intuitive and emotional nature, traits that will guide you through the coming year.

The year begins with a promising Jupiter-Pluto trine on June 2nd, indicating a period of power and influence in your career. This aspect suggests that your hard work and determination will pay off, leading to significant progress in your professional life. You may find yourself taking on more responsibilities and making important decisions that will shape your career path. This is a time for you to step into your power and assert your leadership skills.

However, the semi-square between Venus and Saturn on June 8th suggests some financial challenges. You may need to tighten your belt and make some tough decisions regarding your finances. But remember, Cancer, these challenges are temporary and are meant to strengthen your financial management skills. It's a time to reassess your financial habits and make necessary changes.

The trine between Venus and Jupiter on December 19th will bring a much-needed relief from financial stress. This aspect indicates a period of financial growth and abundance. You may receive a job offer, a promotion, or an unexpected financial gain around this time. This is a time to celebrate your achievements and enjoy the fruits of your labor.

In terms of relationships, the conjunction between Mercury and Venus on June 17th suggests a period of harmony and understanding. You will find it easier to express your thoughts and feelings, leading to stronger and more meaningful relationships. This is a time for deep conversations and mutual understanding. You may find that your relationships are strengthened during this period.

However, the square between Mercury and the True Node on June 22nd indicates some conflicts in your social life. You may find yourself at odds with your friends or social group. Remember, Cancer, it's okay to disagree. Use your natural diplomatic skills to navigate these conflicts. This is a time to stand up for your beliefs and values, even if it means going against the crowd.

The sextile between Venus and Chiron on December 23rd brings healing energy to your relationships. This is a good time to mend broken relationships and let go of any grudges you've been holding onto. This is a time for forgiveness and reconciliation. You may find that your relationships are healed and strengthened during this period.

The semi-sextile between Mars and Jupiter on June 15th suggests a period of high energy and vitality. This is a great time to start a new fitness regimen or to push yourself in your current workouts. Your energy levels will be high during this period, making it a great time to push your physical limits.

However, the square between the Sun and Neptune on June 20th warns of potential health issues related to stress or exhaustion. Make sure to take care of your mental health during this time and don't hesitate to seek help if needed. This is a time to prioritize self-care and ensure that you are taking care of your mental and emotional health.

The trine between Mercury and Saturn on June 26th brings a period of stability and balance in your health. This is a good time to focus on building healthy habits and routines. This is a time for you to take control of your health and make positive changes in your lifestyle.

The quintile between the Sun and the True Node on June 3rd indicates a period of spiritual growth and self-discovery. This is a great time to explore new spiritual practices or to deepen your existing ones. You may find yourself drawn to meditation, yoga, or other spiritual practices. This is a time for introspection and self-discovery. You may find that you gain new insights into yourself and the world around you.

The semi-square between Mercury and Uranus on June 22nd suggests a period of sudden insights and revelations. You may experience a shift in your beliefs or perspectives during this time. This is a time for you to challenge your old beliefs and open yourself up to new ideas. You may find that you see the world in a new light after this period.

The quintile between Jupiter and the True Node on December 13th brings a period of personal growth and expansion. This is a great time to set new personal goals and to push yourself out of your comfort zone. This is a time for you to challenge yourself and strive for personal growth. You may find that you are capable of more than you thought possible.

In conclusion, Cancer, 2024 is a year of growth and transformation. While there will be challenges along the way, remember that these are opportunities for growth and learning. Embrace the changes and trust that the universe is guiding you towards your highest good. This is a year for you to step into your power and realize your full potential. Remember, Cancer, you are intuitive and emotional, and you have the skills and abilities to navigate any challenges that come your way. Here's to a year of growth, transformation, and success.

January 2024

Horoscope

In January 2024, Cancer, you can expect a month filled with a mix of challenges and opportunities. The astrological aspects during this time will influence various areas of your life, urging you to adapt, communicate effectively, and make balanced decisions.

As the month begins, Venus squares Saturn on January 1st, creating a sense of tension and restriction in your personal relationships. You may find it challenging to express your affections, and there could be a need to reevaluate the dynamics within your connections. It's crucial to maintain open and honest communication with your loved ones, finding a delicate balance between your need for independence and your commitment to your relationships.

On January 3rd, Venus forms a quincunx aspect with Jupiter, presenting some adjustments and challenges in matters of the heart. This aspect may require you to reassess your desires and make compromises to maintain harmony in your romantic relationships. Patience, understanding, and clear communication will be key to navigating these adjustments successfully.

In terms of communication and intellectual pursuits, January 3rd brings a quintile aspect between Mercury and Saturn. This alignment favors structured communication, making it an excellent time for focused discussions and planning. Your thoughts and ideas may flow with clarity, allowing you to express yourself effectively in both personal and professional spheres.

Throughout January, it's important to pay attention to the balance between your personal and professional lives. The aspects indicate a need to prioritize self-care, emotional well-being, and responsible financial management. By finding equilibrium between your various responsibilities and commitments, you can navigate the month with greater ease and success.

Remember, Cancer, that change is a natural part of life. Embracing the unexpected and being open to new opportunities will lead to personal growth and positive outcomes. Despite the challenges that may arise, your ability to adapt, communicate effectively, and maintain balance will ultimately guide you towards a fulfilling and transformative month.

Love

Love and relationships may encounter a few challenges and opportunities in January 2024, Cancer. The astrological aspects during this month encourage you to communicate openly, make adjustments, and find a balance between your personal desires and the needs of your partner.

The square aspect between Venus and Saturn on January 1st may create a sense of emotional distance or restrictiveness in your relationships. You may feel the need to protect your emotions or struggle to express your affections. It's crucial to address these feelings honestly and engage in open conversations with your loved ones. By acknowledging your concerns and listening to the perspective of your partner, you can work towards finding a middle ground that supports the growth of your relationship.

On January 3rd, Venus forms a quincunx aspect with Jupiter, presenting challenges that require adjustments and compromises in matters of the heart. You might have conflicting desires or differing expectations within your romantic connections. This aspect emphasizes the importance of active communication, understanding, and flexibility. By being willing to meet your partner halfway and finding common ground, you can foster a sense of harmony and strengthen your bond.

For single Cancer individuals, this is a time to explore your own desires and make sure you are clear on what you truly want in a relationship. Avoid rushing into commitments or compromising your values. Take this opportunity to focus on self-love, personal growth, and building a strong foundation within yourself.

Throughout the month, it's important to remember that healthy relationships require both individuals to express their needs and feelings openly. By fostering an atmosphere of trust, understanding, and compromise, you can navigate the challenges and embrace the opportunities for growth and deeper connections in your love life.

Career

January 2024 presents several favorable aspects that will impact your career, Cancer. The astrological influences during this month encourage you to embrace change, pursue innovative ideas, and approach your professional goals with discipline and determination.

The Sun's trine with Uranus on January 9th brings unexpected opportunities and a fresh perspective to your career path. This aspect sparks your creativity and prompts you to think outside the box. Embrace any unique ideas or unconventional approaches that arise during this time, as they may lead to significant breakthroughs and advancements in your professional life.

On the same day, Mars forms a sextile with Saturn, providing you with the stamina, discipline, and focus needed to excel in your work. This alignment strengthens your ability to tackle tasks efficiently and effectively. You'll find that your hard work and dedication pay off, as you make notable progress towards your career goals.

Throughout January, it's essential to maintain a balance between your personal and professional lives. Prioritize self-care and ensure that you take time for rest and rejuvenation. Remember that a healthy work-life balance is vital for long-term success and overall well-being.

This month also encourages you to establish a strong foundation in your professional endeavors. Focus on enhancing your skills, seeking opportunities for growth, and nurturing positive relationships with colleagues and superiors. Networking and collaboration can play a significant role in expanding your professional horizons and opening doors to new possibilities.

Finance

In terms of finances, January 2024 demands careful planning, responsible decision-making, and a focus on long-term stability, Cancer. The astrological aspects during this month emphasize the need for caution and strategic financial management.

The semi-square aspect between the Sun and Saturn on January 9th serves as a reminder to be mindful of your spending habits and exercise restraint. Avoid impulsive purchases and evaluate the long-term value of your financial choices. This aspect calls for responsible money management and a realistic approach to your financial goals.

Additionally, the semi-square between Saturn and the True Node on January 15th highlights the importance of making informed decisions and avoiding risky investments. Take the time to thoroughly research any financial opportunities that come your way. Seek professional advice if needed, as this can provide valuable insights and guidance for navigating your financial matters.

During this month, it's crucial to establish a solid foundation for your financial well-being. This includes creating a budget, setting achievable savings goals, and prioritizing financial stability. Consider reviewing your current investments and reassessing your long-term financial plans. Taking a conservative approach and focusing on building a secure financial future will serve you well.

Remember to practice patience and avoid comparing your financial situation to others. Each individual's financial journey is unique, and it's important to focus on your own progress and growth. By maintaining a disciplined and cautious approach to your finances, you can lay the groundwork for future prosperity and financial security.

While the emphasis during this month is on responsible financial management, it's also important to find a balance between financial stability and enjoying life. Allocate some resources towards experiences that bring you joy and fulfillment. By practicing mindfulness in your financial decisions and finding that equilibrium, you can navigate January 2024 with greater confidence and peace of mind.

Health

Your well-being takes center stage in January 2024, Cancer. The astrological aspects during this month highlight the importance of paying attention to your physical and emotional health. It's crucial to prioritize self-care, address any lingering issues, and cultivate a holistic approach to your well-being.

The square aspect between the Sun and Chiron on January 6th may bring up emotional and physical wounds that require healing. Take this opportunity to engage in introspection, seek support if needed, and work towards resolving any unresolved issues. Emotional well-being is just as important as physical health, so make sure to address any underlying emotional imbalances or trauma.

On January 15th, the semi-square aspect between the Sun and Neptune may lead to confusion or a lack of clarity in matters of health. It's important to rely on trusted sources of information and be discerning about the advice you receive. Stick to established self-care routines, prioritize rest, and be cautious of any new health regimens or practices that seem too good to be true.

Throughout the month, establish a self-care routine that supports your overall well-being. This includes nourishing your body with nutritious food, engaging in regular physical activity, and prioritizing restful sleep. Incorporate stress-management techniques such as meditation, deep breathing exercises, or engaging in activities that bring you joy and relaxation.

Listening to your body's signals is crucial during this time. Pay attention to any signs of fatigue, stress, or discomfort, and take appropriate measures to address them. Consult with healthcare professionals if necessary and be proactive in seeking the support and guidance you need to maintain your health.

Travel

While January 2024 does not highlight significant travel-related aspects for Cancer, it's essential to approach any travel plans with thorough preparation and flexibility. The astrological influences during this month may bring some unpredictability or changes to your travel arrangements.

If you have any planned journeys, ensure that all necessary details and logistics are well-organized. Double-check your travel itineraries, reservations, and travel documents to avoid any last-minute surprises. Allow extra time for unexpected delays or changes in your plans, as the astrological aspects indicate a possibility of unforeseen circumstances.

Flexibility and adaptability will be your allies during this time. Keep an open mind and be prepared to adjust your travel plans if needed. Embrace any unexpected detours or changes as opportunities for adventure and growth.

If you have no specific travel plans, consider exploring local destinations or taking short day trips to recharge and rejuvenate. Engaging in nature walks, visiting nearby parks, or taking a short break from your usual routine can provide a sense of refreshment and relaxation.

Insight from the stars

The stars this January whisper a tale of balance for Cancerians. Your nurturing nature is a gift but remember not to neglect yourself in the process. This month is about setting foundations in love, career, and personal development. Listen to your intuition, but also make well-thought-out plans. The stars are aligned to offer you a fresh start. Embrace it with open arms and a wise heart.

Best days of the month: January   9th, 12th, 19th, 26th, 28th, 29th and 30th.

February 2024

Horoscope

February 2024 brings a dynamic and transformative energy for Cancer, as the astrological aspects influence various aspects of your life. This month encourages self-reflection, emotional healing, and the pursuit of personal growth. With a focus on relationships, career, finances, health, and travel, you will navigate through February with determination, adaptability, and a willingness to embrace change.

In matters of the heart, Cancer, this month presents a mixed bag of energies. The semi-sextile between the Sun and Venus on February 5th brings a gentle influence of harmony and balance to your love life. It encourages you to find a middle ground between your own desires and the needs of your partner. Communication and compromise will play essential roles in maintaining healthy and harmonious relationships.

However, the square aspect between Venus and Chiron on the same day may bring some emotional wounds to the surface. This aspect invites you to heal past hurts and unresolved issues in your relationships. Use this opportunity to engage in open and honest conversations with your partner and address any lingering conflicts. By nurturing emotional healing, you can foster stronger and more authentic connections.

In summary, February 2024 is a transformative month for Cancer, encompassing various aspects of your life. Embrace the healing energy in your relationships, seize career opportunities, practice responsible financial management, prioritize self-care, and approach travel with flexibility. By navigating through the month with resilience, adaptability, and a willingness to embrace change, you will pave the way for personal growth and a deeper sense of fulfillment.

Love

Love and relationships take center stage for Cancer in February 2024. The astrological aspects during this month bring a mix of harmonious energies and emotional healing opportunities, urging you to deepen connections and address any unresolved issues.

On February 5th, the semi-sextile aspect between the Sun and Venus brings a gentle and supportive influence to your love life. This alignment encourages compromise, cooperation, and finding a balance between your own needs and the desires of your partner. It's a favorable time to express your affections and nurture the emotional bonds within your relationships.

However, the square aspect between Venus and Chiron on the same day may bring up emotional wounds or past hurts within your relationships. This aspect invites you to confront and heal these issues, fostering a greater sense of emotional well-being and authenticity within your connections. Engaging in open and honest communication with your partner will be essential during this time.

For single Cancer individuals, this month encourages self-reflection and self-love. Take the opportunity to heal any emotional wounds from the past and focus on personal growth. By cultivating a strong sense of self and addressing any unresolved issues, you pave the way for attracting a more fulfilling and healthy romantic partnership in the future.

Remember that love is a journey of growth and understanding. By nurturing open and honest communication, practicing empathy and compassion, and being willing to address and heal emotional wounds, you can deepen your connections and create a more harmonious and fulfilling love life.

Career

February 2024 presents opportunities for professional growth and advancement for Cancer individuals. The astrological aspects during this month encourage assertiveness, cooperation, and embracing new challenges in your career.

The conjunction between Venus and Mars on February 22nd brings a harmonious blend of assertiveness and collaboration to your professional sphere. This alignment favors working in teams, fostering positive relationships with colleagues, and undertaking new projects with confidence. Your ability to assert yourself and take on leadership roles will be supported during this time.

Additionally, the quintile aspect between Mercury and Jupiter on the same day expands your intellectual capacity and enhances your problem-solving abilities. You may find yourself inspired by new ideas and innovative approaches in your work. Embrace these opportunities to expand your skill set and contribute valuable insights to your projects or team.

Throughout the month, it's important to maintain a proactive approach to your career. Seek out learning opportunities, whether through training programs, workshops, or mentorship. Cultivate positive relationships with superiors and colleagues, as they may provide valuable support and guidance.

Remember to set clear goals and intentions for your professional growth. Use the favorable aspects to assert yourself, take on new challenges, and embrace opportunities for advancement. By combining your assertiveness with a collaborative mindset and a willingness to learn and grow, you can make significant strides in your career during February 2024.

Finance

Financial matters require careful planning and discernment for Cancer individuals in February 2024. The astrological aspects during this month remind you to prioritize stability, exercise caution, and make informed decisions regarding your finances.

The square aspect between Venus and Jupiter on February 24th may bring temptations to indulge in impulsive spending or take unnecessary risks with your money. It's important to exercise caution and ensure that your financial choices align with your long-term goals. Take the time to evaluate the potential risks and rewards of any investments or financial decisions you make.

This month calls for responsible financial management. Review your budget, prioritize savings, and ensure that your expenses align with your income. Seek professional advice if needed, as an objective perspective can provide valuable insights and guidance for your financial journey.

Consider exploring ways to enhance your financial stability and security. This may involve diversifying your income streams, seeking opportunities for passive income, or investing in long-term assets. Adopt a long-term perspective when it comes to your finances, prioritizing stability and sustainable growth over short-term gains.

Remember that financial well-being is not just about accumulating wealth but also about achieving a sense of security and peace of mind. By making thoughtful and informed financial decisions, you can lay the foundation for long-term prosperity and financial freedom.

Health

February 2024 emphasizes the importance of self-care and emotional well-being for Cancer individuals. The astrological aspects during this month encourage you to prioritize your health, address any underlying imbalances, and engage in activities that promote both physical and emotional well-being.

The semi-sextile between the Sun and Neptune on February 15th invites you to incorporate relaxation techniques and mindfulness practices into your daily routine. Engage in activities such as meditation, yoga, or spending time in nature to promote a sense of inner peace and tranquility. Take the time to listen to your body's signals and address any physical or emotional imbalances promptly.

Emotional well-being plays a crucial role in your overall health. The square aspect between Venus and Chiron on February 5th may bring up past emotional wounds or unresolved issues. Use this opportunity to engage in self-reflection, seek support if needed, and work towards healing these emotional wounds. Consider exploring therapy, counseling, or holistic practices to support your emotional well-being.

It's important to maintain a balanced approach to your health. Focus on nourishing your body with nutritious food, engaging in regular physical activity, and prioritizing restful sleep. Establishing a self-care routine that includes these elements will contribute to your overall vitality and well-being.

Remember to listen to your body's needs and practice self-compassion. If you're experiencing any persistent physical symptoms or health concerns, seek professional medical advice. Prioritize your health and

well-being as a foundation for a fulfilling and vibrant
life.

Travel

February 2024 invites Cancer individuals to
approach travel plans with adaptability and an open
mind. While the astrological aspects during this month
don't specifically highlight significant travel
influences, it's important to embrace any unexpected
changes or detours that may arise during your journeys.

Maintain flexibility in your travel plans and be
prepared for unexpected delays or alterations. Embrace
these changes as opportunities for new experiences and
personal growth. A willingness to adapt and go with
the flow will make your travel experiences more
enjoyable and enriching.

If you have no specific travel plans, consider
exploring local destinations or taking short day trips to
recharge and rejuvenate. Engaging in nature walks,
visiting nearby parks, or immersing yourself in local
cultural activities can provide a sense of adventure and
relaxation.

During your travels, prioritize self-care and well-
being. Take breaks when needed, stay hydrated, and
prioritize restful sleep. Engage in mindfulness

practices to stay grounded and fully immerse yourself in the present moment.

Insight from the stars

Embrace the changes that come your way, for they bring opportunities for evolution. Remember, your emotional intelligence is your strength, and your empathy is your guide. Stay open to new perspectives, maintain balance in your relationships, and nurture your physical and emotional health. This is a time for you to shine, dear Crab, in all your lunar radiance.

Best days of the month: February 5th, 15th, 19th, 22nd, 24th, 27th, and 29th.

March 2024

Horoscope

March 2024 brings a mix of emotional depth, spiritual exploration, and opportunities for personal growth for Cancer individuals. The astrological aspects during this month encourage self-reflection, emotional healing, and a reconnection with your inner self.

The Sun's sextile with Jupiter on March 1st sets the tone for the month, promoting optimism, expansion, and a sense of adventure. You may feel a renewed enthusiasm and a desire to explore new possibilities in various areas of your life.

Mercury's semi-sextile with Mars on the same day enhances your communication skills and mental agility. This alignment supports productive conversations, assertiveness, and taking action on your ideas and plans.

Venus's sextile with Chiron on March 1st encourages you to explore your emotional wounds and engage in healing practices. This alignment invites you to embrace vulnerability, seek support, and work towards emotional well-being.

Throughout the month, the conjunction between Mercury and Neptune on March 8th enhances your intuition, imagination, and creativity. This alignment empowers you to tap into your spiritual side and explore artistic pursuits or engage in practices that deepen your connection with the divine.

March 18th brings a conjunction between Mercury and the True Node, signaling a significant turning point in your personal growth. This alignment invites you to align your communication and thoughts with your life's purpose, allowing you to express your authentic self and make decisions that support your soul's journey.

The Sun's sextile with Pluto on March 21st further empowers your personal transformation. It's a time to embrace your personal power, let go of old patterns, and initiate positive change in your life.

Throughout the month, Venus's conjunction with Saturn on March 21st invites you to explore the balance between love and responsibility. This alignment supports commitment and stability in your relationships while encouraging you to set healthy boundaries and take responsibility for your own emotional well-being.

The month ends with Mars quintile Jupiter on March 28th, amplifying your enthusiasm, motivation, and desire for growth. This aspect fuels your ambitions and encourages you to take bold actions towards your goals.

In summary, March 2024 offers Cancer individuals a powerful journey of self-discovery, emotional healing, and personal growth. Embrace the opportunities for expansion, tap into your intuition, and engage in practices that nourish your mind, body, and soul. By aligning with your purpose, embracing vulnerability, and nurturing your relationships, you can make significant strides on your journey towards a more fulfilling and authentic life.

Love

In matters of the heart, March 2024 encourages Cancer individuals to explore their emotional depths, prioritize self-love, and embrace vulnerability within their relationships. The astrological aspects during this month invite you to deepen your emotional connections, heal past wounds, and foster a greater sense of authenticity and intimacy.

The Venus sextile with Chiron on March 1st sets the tone for the month, encouraging emotional healing and self-reflection within your relationships. This alignment invites you to address any emotional wounds and work towards greater self-acceptance and self-love. By doing so, you create a solid foundation for more fulfilling and intimate connections with your partner.

The Venus conjunction with Saturn on March 21st brings a sense of commitment and responsibility to your relationships. This alignment emphasizes the importance of setting healthy boundaries, establishing trust, and nurturing long-term stability. It's a favorable time to solidify your commitment or take a more serious approach to your romantic partnership.

Throughout the month, communication plays a vital role in your love life. The conjunction between Mercury and the True Node on March 18th enhances your ability to express your true feelings and align your communication with your soul's purpose. This alignment supports heartfelt conversations, deepening understanding, and fostering emotional connection with your partner.

Embracing vulnerability and open-heartedness is key to strengthening your relationships during this time. The Sun's semi-sextile with Chiron on March 7th

encourages you to acknowledge and share your
emotional vulnerabilities, allowing for a deeper level
of trust and intimacy.

Career

The astrological aspects during this month
encourage you to embrace your ambitions,
communicate with confidence, and pursue new
avenues for success.

The Mercury semi-sextile with Mars on March 1st
enhances your communication skills and mental agility
in the professional sphere. This alignment empowers
you to express your ideas, take decisive action, and
assert yourself confidently in the workplace.

The Mercury conjunction with the True Node on
March 18th marks a significant turning point in your
career journey. This alignment invites you to align
your communication and thoughts with your life's
purpose, allowing you to make career decisions that
support your soul's growth. Pay attention to
synchronicities and intuitive guidance, as they may
lead you towards new opportunities and paths for
professional advancement.

Throughout the month, it's essential to be proactive
and assertive in pursuing your career goals. The Mars
sextile with the True Node on March 4th fuels your

ambition and encourages you to take bold actions towards your aspirations. Seize opportunities for growth, network with influential individuals, and trust in your abilities to make a positive impact in your chosen field.

The Sun's semi-square with Uranus on March 9th brings a burst of innovative energy to your career endeavors. Embrace change, think outside the box, and be open to unconventional approaches. This aspect supports your ability to adapt to new challenges and break through any professional limitations.

Remember to communicate your ideas, visions, and ambitions with clarity and confidence. The Mercury conjunction with Chiron on March 20th enhances your ability to express your true self and communicate your authentic desires. Use this alignment to advocate for yourself, seek opportunities for advancement, and engage in meaningful collaborations.

Finance

March 2024 brings a focus on financial stability, responsible decision-making, and the potential for financial growth for Cancer individuals. The astrological aspects during this month encourage you to assess your financial situation, make informed choices, and create a solid foundation for long-term prosperity.

The Venus square with Uranus on March 3rd calls for caution in financial matters. This alignment warns against impulsive spending or risky investments. It's important to approach financial decisions with careful consideration and avoid unnecessary risks during this time.

The Venus conjunction with Saturn on March 21st brings a sense of responsibility and discipline to your financial endeavors. This alignment encourages you to establish a budget, set financial goals, and prioritize long-term stability. By being diligent and disciplined in your financial practices, you can create a strong foundation for future financial growth.

Throughout the month, pay attention to your financial instincts and trust your intuition when making financial decisions. The Mercury conjunction with Neptune on March 8th enhances your intuitive abilities and encourages you to listen to your inner wisdom when it comes to financial matters. Trust your gut feelings and seek guidance from trusted financial advisors if needed.

The Mars semi-square with Pluto on March 25th serves as a reminder to approach financial power dynamics with caution. Be mindful of any manipulative or controlling influences in your financial interactions and take steps to protect your financial interests.

It's important to cultivate a balanced approach to your finances, focusing on both saving and investing. The Venus sextile with Jupiter on March 24th presents opportunities for financial growth and expansion. This alignment encourages you to be open to new possibilities and seek out investments or ventures that have the potential for long-term prosperity.

Remember to practice gratitude and abundance consciousness when it comes to your finances. By focusing on what you already have and appreciating the abundance in your life, you attract more opportunities for financial growth and stability.

Health

In terms of health and well-being, March 2024 encourages Cancer individuals to prioritize self-care, emotional well-being, and a holistic approach to their overall health. The astrological aspects during this month highlight the importance of finding balance, managing stress, and nurturing both the body and mind.

The Sun's semi-sextile with Chiron on March 7th invites you to address any emotional wounds that may be affecting your physical well-being. Take time for self-reflection, engage in healing practices, and seek support if needed. By nurturing your emotional health, you can create a solid foundation for overall well-being.

The Mars sextile with Neptune on March 19th supports a holistic approach to health. This alignment encourages you to explore alternative therapies, engage in mindful practices, and prioritize self-care rituals that nurture both your body and spirit. Incorporating activities such as yoga, meditation, or nature walks can have a positive impact on your overall well-being.

Throughout the month, it's important to manage stress and find healthy outlets for emotional release. The Sun's conjunction with Neptune on March 17th invites you to prioritize rest, relaxation, and rejuvenation. Listen to your body's needs and give yourself permission to take breaks when necessary.

Maintaining a balanced lifestyle is key to your well-being during this time. The Venus conjunction with Saturn on March 21st encourages you to establish healthy routines, including regular exercise, proper nutrition, and sufficient sleep. By creating a foundation of self-care and balance, you can enhance your overall vitality and energy levels.

Be mindful of any tendencies to overwork or neglect your own needs. The Mercury conjunction with Mars on March 22nd serves as a reminder to find a healthy work-life balance and prioritize self-care. Avoid excessive stress or burnout by setting boundaries and practicing self-compassion.

Remember to listen to your body's signals and seek medical advice if needed. Pay attention to any recurring health issues and take proactive steps to address them. Trust your intuition when it comes to your health, and seek guidance from trusted healthcare professionals to ensure optimal well-being.

Travel

March 2024 presents Cancer individuals with opportunities for travel, exploration, and expanding their horizons. The astrological aspects during this month encourage you to embrace new experiences, seek adventure, and broaden your perspectives through travel.

The Mars sextile with the True Node on March 4th ignites your sense of adventure and encourages you to take bold steps towards exploring new destinations. Whether it's a spontaneous weekend getaway or a more extended trip, this alignment supports travel plans that align with your personal growth and expansion.

The Sun's semi-sextile with Uranus on March 9th brings a sense of excitement and openness to new experiences. Embrace unexpected opportunities or invitations for travel that come your way during this time. It's a favorable period for embracing change and embracing new cultures, customs, and perspectives.

Throughout the month, it's important to balance your desire for exploration with practicality and responsibility. The Venus conjunction with Saturn on March 21st encourages you to plan and organize your travel arrangements carefully. This alignment reminds you to consider your budget, prioritize safety, and ensure that your travel plans align with your long-term goals.

As you embark on your travels, take time to immerse yourself in the local culture, connect with the people you encounter, and embrace new experiences. Engage in activities that expand your knowledge and broaden your perspectives. Whether it's trying new cuisines, exploring historical sites, or engaging in outdoor adventures, allow yourself to fully embrace the richness of the travel experience.

It's also essential to prioritize self-care and maintain a sense of balance while traveling. The Mars semi-square with Pluto on March 25th reminds you to be mindful of power dynamics and potentially challenging situations. Practice self-awareness, trust your intuition, and prioritize your safety and well-being at all times.

Insight from the stars

The stars speak of a balance between dreaming and doing for Cancer in March 2024. Embrace your emotional depth and intuitive insight but remember to ground them in practical action. This is a time for personal growth and exploration, both within your relationships and in your journey with self. The cosmos encourages you to dream big, but also to take concrete steps towards realizing those dreams. Remember, dear Crab, you are the master of your own destiny.

Best days of the month: March 4th, 7th, 17th, 18th, 21st, 24th and 28th.

April 2024

Horoscope

April brings a mix of energetic and transformative influences for Cancer individuals. As the Sun moves through Aries, the focus is on self-expression, personal growth, and taking charge of your life. You may feel a surge of confidence and assertiveness, motivating you to pursue your goals and assert your needs. However, be mindful of the semi-square between the Sun and Saturn on April 2nd, which could create some tension and obstacles. Use this as an opportunity to assess your responsibilities and make necessary adjustments. The Sun's conjunction with Neptune on April 3rd encourages you to tap into your intuition and engage in spiritual practices for inner guidance. Additionally, the Mars quintile Uranus on April 3rd sparks creativity and the desire for freedom and individuality. Embrace these energies to initiate positive changes in your life.

Love

In love matters, April brings a dynamic blend of passion and emotional depth. The Venus-Neptune conjunction on April 3rd heightens romantic and dreamy vibes, fostering a deep emotional connection with your partner. It's a favorable time to express your love through creative gestures and heartfelt conversations. However, the semi-square between Venus and Jupiter on April 8th may create some challenges in relationships, particularly regarding differences in values and beliefs. Open communication and understanding will be key to finding common ground and maintaining harmony. Single Cancer individuals may experience an intense attraction to someone new, but it's important to balance passion with practicality and ensure compatibility on a deeper level.

Career

Career-wise, April presents opportunities for growth and assertiveness. The Sun's conjunction with Chiron on April 8th empowers you to embrace your unique skills and talents, showcasing your abilities to superiors and colleagues. This can lead to recognition and advancement in your professional sphere.

However, the Mars conjunction with Saturn on April
10th indicates the need for patience and perseverance.
Challenges and delays may arise, requiring you to stay
focused and determined in pursuing your goals. The
Mars sextile Jupiter on April 19th brings positive
energy and opportunities for expansion. Take
calculated risks and seize favorable prospects that align
with your long-term career objectives.

Finance

Financially, April calls for a balanced approach and
mindful decision-making. The Venus-Pluto sextile on
April 6th encourages you to assess your financial
strategies and make necessary adjustments for stability
and long-term growth. However, the semi-square
between Venus and Jupiter on April 8th warns against
impulsive spending or taking unnecessary risks. Be
prudent and consider the bigger picture when making
financial decisions. The Venus-Neptune semi-sextile
on April 28th reminds you to trust your intuition and
seek financial advice from reliable sources. Avoid
hasty investments and focus on practical, well-
researched opportunities that align with your financial
goals.

Health

In terms of health, April highlights the importance of maintaining a balance between physical and emotional well-being. The Sun's semi-sextile with Saturn on April 2nd serves as a reminder to establish a routine that prioritizes self-care and discipline. Incorporate regular exercise, nutritious meals, and sufficient rest into your daily life. The Mars-Neptune conjunction on April 29th calls for restorative practices such as meditation, yoga, or spending time in nature to replenish your energy levels. Take time to address any emotional stressors and seek support if needed. Focus on maintaining a positive mindset and nurturing your overall well-being.

Travel

April offers favorable opportunities for travel and exploration. The Mars-Jupiter sextile on April 19th ignites a sense of adventure and curiosity, urging you to explore new places and cultures. Whether it's a short weekend getaway or a longer vacation, embrace the spirit of adventure and expand your horizons. Travel can provide inspiration, broaden your perspective, and rejuvenate your spirit. Take precautions and plan accordingly to ensure smooth and safe travel experiences. If international travel is not feasible, consider exploring local destinations or engaging in virtual experiences that allow you to satisfy your wanderlust.

Insight from the stars

"Believe in your abilities and showcase your unique talents. Your confidence will attract opportunities for advancement."

Best days of the month: April 2nd, 8th, 10th, 19th, 21st, 28th, and 29th.

May 2024

Horoscope

May brings a mix of transformative and communicative energies for Cancer individuals. As the Sun moves into Taurus, the focus is on stability, practicality, and effective communication. This month encourages you to ground yourself, set clear boundaries, and express your thoughts and feelings with clarity. The square between Venus and Pluto on May 1st may bring some intensity and power struggles in relationships, but it also provides an opportunity for transformation and growth. Use this time to delve into deeper emotional connections and address any underlying issues. The Mars sextile Pluto on May 3rd ignites your passion and determination, empowering you to overcome obstacles and make significant progress in your personal and professional life.

Love

In love matters, May highlights the importance of open and honest communication in relationships. The Sun's semi-square with Neptune on May 3rd may create some confusion or idealistic expectations. It's essential to have clear and heartfelt conversations with your partner to avoid misunderstandings and ensure that both of your needs and desires are understood. This is a time to be realistic and practical about your romantic connections. Reflect on your emotional boundaries and make sure they are healthy and respected. The Sun's conjunction with Uranus on May 13th brings unexpected shifts and excitement in your love life. Embrace the spontaneity and be open to new experiences. It's a time to explore uncharted territories in relationships, try new activities together, and deepen your connection through shared adventures. Single Cancer individuals may find themselves drawn to intellectual and stimulating conversations that lead to meaningful connections. Keep an open mind and engage in social activities where you can meet like-minded individuals who share your interests and values.

Career

Career-wise, May presents opportunities for effective communication and professional growth. The Mercury-Chiron conjunction on May 6th enhances your communication skills and empowers you to express yourself with authenticity and compassion. This can lead to improved relationships with colleagues and superiors, fostering a positive work environment. Use this time to share your ideas, contribute to team projects, and showcase your unique talents. The Venus-Uranus conjunction on May 18th brings innovative ideas and fresh perspectives in your career. Embrace changes and be open to new opportunities that may come your way. This is a favorable time to network and expand your professional connections. Attend industry events, engage in professional development courses, and seek mentors who can guide you towards new horizons. The Mars-Pluto sextile on May 18th empowers you with determination and drive, allowing you to overcome challenges and make significant progress in your professional endeavors. Harness this transformative energy to tackle ambitious projects, assert your leadership skills, and make a positive impact within your workplace.

Finance

Financially, May encourages you to take a practical
and disciplined approach. The Venus-Neptune semi-
square on May 10th advises caution in financial
matters. Avoid impulsive spending and take time to
assess the practicality and long-term value of your
investments. It's crucial to have a budget in place and
prioritize your financial goals. Consider seeking advice
from financial experts or exploring new avenues for
increasing your income. The Venus-Jupiter sextile on
May 23rd brings positive energy and opportunities for
financial growth. It's a favorable time to evaluate your
financial strategy and make adjustments as needed.
Focus on long-term stability and avoid making hasty
financial decisions based on short-term gains. By
maintaining a practical and disciplined approach to
your finances, you can build a solid foundation for
future prosperity.

Health

In terms of health, May emphasizes the importance
of self-care and maintaining balance. The Sun's semi-
square with Chiron on May 27th may bring up
emotional wounds or sensitivities. Take time to address
and heal any emotional stressors, seeking support from

loved ones or professional therapists if needed. Prioritize self-care activities that nurture your mind, body, and soul. Incorporate relaxation techniques such as meditation, deep breathing exercises, or indulging in activities that bring you joy and calmness. Nourish your body with nutritious meals, engage in regular physical exercise, and prioritize sufficient rest to maintain overall well-being. Focus on establishing healthy routines that support your mental and emotional well-being, allowing you to navigate any challenges with resilience and inner strength.

Travel

May offers opportunities for travel and exploration, particularly with the Sun's trine to Pluto on May 22nd. This aspect brings a sense of adventure and empowerment, making it an ideal time to plan a trip or engage in activities that broaden your horizons. Whether it's a short getaway or a longer vacation, embrace the transformative energy and use travel as a means to expand your perspective and discover new cultures and experiences. Explore destinations that offer a blend of relaxation and exploration, allowing you to unwind while also satisfying your curiosity. If travel is not feasible, consider exploring local destinations or indulging in virtual experiences that allow you to satisfy your wanderlust. Engage in activities that stimulate your mind, such as visiting museums, attending workshops, or immersing yourself in nature. Use these experiences as opportunities for personal growth and self-discovery.

Insight from the stars

This is a time to delve into your subconscious, heal your emotional wounds, and prepare for the upcoming personal new year when the Sun enters your sign. Remember, dear Crab, self-care is not selfish but an essential part of your journey. Nourish your mind, body, and soul this month.

Best days of the month: May 8th, 13th, 18th, 22nd, 23rd, 28th and 31st.

June 2024

Horoscope

In June, Cancer individuals will experience a dynamic and transformative month that will bring both challenges and opportunities. The celestial movements urge you to focus on self-care, nurturing your relationships, and aligning your actions with your long-term goals. It's a time of personal growth and self-discovery, as you tap into your intuition and make important decisions for your future.

The month begins with Mars in Aries, forming a semi-sextile with Uranus in Taurus. This alignment encourages you to embrace change and take bold steps towards your aspirations. It's a time to break free from old patterns and explore new possibilities. However, be mindful of impulsive actions and ensure that your choices align with your values and long-term goals.

The Sun's quintile with Neptune on June 1 enhances your intuition and imagination, opening doors to creative and spiritual pursuits. This aspect inspires you to trust your instincts and engage in activities that bring you joy and fulfillment.

As the month progresses, Venus enters Gemini on June 2, adding a touch of charm and flirtation to your love life. Venus' quintile with Neptune on June 6 intensifies your romantic energy, fostering deep emotional connections and enhancing your intuition in matters of the heart. It's a time to express your feelings and nurture your relationships.

Mercury, the planet of communication, moves into Cancer on June 17, amplifying your ability to express your thoughts and emotions. Mercury's square with Chiron on June 28 may bring some challenges in communication, requiring you to be patient and compassionate with yourself and others. Practice active listening and choose your words carefully to avoid misunderstandings.

Love

In the realm of love, June brings a mix of passion, romance, and emotional growth for Cancer individuals. With Venus in Gemini, you'll experience a heightened desire for intellectual connection and stimulating conversations with your partner. It's an excellent time to deepen your emotional bonds through heartfelt communication and shared experiences.

The Sun's conjunction with Venus on June 14 adds an element of excitement and playfulness to your relationships. Plan romantic dates, surprise your partner with thoughtful gestures, and explore new activities together. This alignment fosters a sense of harmony and mutual understanding in your relationships.

However, Venus' square with Neptune on June 16 may bring some challenges in relationships. Be cautious of idealizing your partner or overlooking red flags. Maintain open and honest communication to ensure clarity and avoid misunderstandings.

For single Cancer individuals, this is a favorable time to meet new people and engage in social activities. The dynamic energy of Mars in Aries fuels your confidence and attractiveness, increasing your chances of forming meaningful connections.

Career

June offers Cancer individuals a promising time for career growth and professional success. The Sun's sextile with Jupiter brings forth a boost of confidence and optimism, empowering you to showcase your unique skills and take on new challenges. It's an opportune moment to set ambitious goals, seek advancement in your current role, or explore new career opportunities. Networking and connecting with influential individuals in your field can prove fruitful. However, it's important to be aware of Mercury's square with Chiron, which may bring some obstacles or self-doubt. Embrace these challenges as opportunities for growth and trust in your abilities. Seek support and guidance from mentors or colleagues to overcome any hurdles and make significant progress in your career. By maintaining a positive mindset and focusing on your long-term objectives, you will attract success and recognition.

Finance

In terms of finances, June advises Cancer individuals to adopt a cautious and disciplined approach. Venus' square with Saturn serves as a reminder to be prudent with your expenses and avoid impulsive purchases. It's crucial to stick to your budget, prioritize essential expenses, and save for future financial stability. This period calls for careful planning and resource management. However, Mars' semi-square with Neptune warns against potential financial risks or deceptive schemes. Exercise caution when making investment decisions and thoroughly research any opportunities before committing your resources. If needed, seek professional advice from a financial expert to ensure you're making informed choices. By maintaining a balanced approach and being mindful of your financial decisions, you can secure your financial well-being and build a solid foundation for the future.

Health

Cancer individuals should prioritize their health and well-being in June. The dynamic planetary influences require you to pay attention to both your physical and emotional health. It's essential to establish a balanced routine that includes regular exercise, nutritious meals, and sufficient rest. Engaging in activities that promote relaxation and stress reduction, such as meditation or yoga, can be beneficial. Be mindful of any signs of burnout or emotional strain, as the demands of work and personal life may be intense. Take time for self-care, engage in activities that bring you joy, and seek support from loved ones when needed. By nurturing your mind, body, and spirit, you'll enhance your overall well-being and maintain resilience in the face of challenges.

Travel

June presents Cancer individuals with opportunities for exciting travel experiences. Whether it's a short getaway or a more extended vacation, this month encourages you to explore new horizons and embrace different cultures. The energy is favorable for connecting with people from diverse backgrounds and expanding your perspective. If you have been contemplating a trip, now is the time to plan and embark on your adventure. However, remember to stay flexible and adaptable, as unforeseen circumstances may arise. Be open to new experiences and embrace the unexpected. Travel can be enriching and offer valuable insights that contribute to your personal growth and broaden your horizons.

Insight from the stars

In June 2024, the stars encourage Cancer to embrace their true self, nurture their relationships, and express their feelings openly. This is a time to assert your identity, showcase your talents, and make your voice heard. Remember, dear Crab, your sensitivity is a strength, not a weakness. Use it to navigate your journey with grace and understanding.

Best days of the month: June 2nd, 10th, 15th, 19th,
22nd, 26th, and 29th

July 2024

Horoscope

July brings a mix of cosmic influences for Cancer individuals, urging you to navigate emotional depths, embrace personal growth, and connect with your inner desires. With the Sun in Cancer, you'll feel a renewed sense of self-awareness and a desire for authenticity.

Emotional exploration takes center stage this month as Jupiter semi-squares Chiron on July 1st, prompting you to confront unresolved emotional wounds. This aspect offers an opportunity for healing and growth, allowing you to release old patterns and embrace a more empowered emotional state. Take time for introspection and seek support from trusted loved ones or professionals if needed.

Mercury's quintile with Mars on July 1st enhances your communication skills and mental agility. You'll find yourself expressing your thoughts with confidence and clarity, making it an excellent time for negotiations, presentations, or engaging in intellectual pursuits.

However, be cautious of the Sun's semi-square with Uranus on July 1st, as it can bring unexpected disruptions or rebellious tendencies. Stay adaptable and open-minded, and be prepared to embrace change if necessary.

July 2nd brings a harmonious trine between Mercury and Neptune, enhancing your intuition and creativity. This aspect supports spiritual pursuits, artistic endeavors, and imaginative thinking. Use this time to delve into your creative projects or connect with your higher self through meditation or dream work.

On July 3rd, Mercury opposes Pluto, intensifying communication dynamics and deepening your understanding of power dynamics. Be mindful of power struggles or manipulative tendencies in your interactions. Focus on maintaining open and honest communication while respecting boundaries.

Love

In matters of the heart, July presents Cancer individuals with opportunities for profound connections and deepening bonds. The trine between Venus and Saturn encourages stability, commitment, and loyalty in relationships. It is a favorable time for taking your love life to the next level.

For those in committed relationships, this is an ideal time to strengthen the foundation of your partnership. Invest time and energy into creating meaningful experiences and nurturing emotional intimacy. Plan romantic dates, engage in heartfelt conversations, and support each other's dreams and aspirations. Building trust and open communication can lead to a more fulfilling and harmonious relationship.

Single Cancer individuals may find themselves attracting a long-term partner who embodies qualities of reliability and security. Embrace the opportunities that come your way and be open to forming meaningful connections. However, remember to listen to your intuition and not rush into commitments. Take the time to truly get to know the other person and ensure compatibility on multiple levels.

Regardless of your relationship status, self-love and self-care are crucial during this period. Nurture your own emotional well-being, engage in activities that bring you joy, and maintain healthy boundaries. By

cultivating a strong sense of self, you attract healthy
and balanced relationships into your life.

Career

Career matters take on significance for Cancer
individuals in July. With Mercury's quintile with Mars,
there is an opportunity to harness your intellectual and
communicative skills to propel your professional
growth.

This is an excellent time to showcase your ideas,
engage in strategic networking, and seek opportunities
for advancement. Your ability to articulate your
thoughts and connect with others can lead to new
collaborations and exciting career prospects. Take the
initiative to express your ambitions and share your
unique insights.

Embrace learning and skill development, as they
play a vital role in your career progression. Seek out
professional development opportunities, attend
workshops or seminars, or enroll in courses that
enhance your expertise. By expanding your knowledge
base, you position yourself as a valuable asset in your
field.

Collaboration and teamwork are also emphasized in
July. Engage in collaborative projects, exchange ideas
with colleagues, and cultivate positive relationships

with your peers. Your ability to work harmoniously within a team can lead to increased productivity and a positive work environment.

It's important to strike a balance between your professional life and personal well-being. Be mindful of maintaining a healthy work-life balance, setting boundaries, and taking breaks when needed. By prioritizing self-care, you can avoid burnout and maintain your productivity and efficiency in the workplace.

Finance

July brings a focus on financial matters for Cancer individuals, urging you to be mindful of your financial well-being. With Venus's square to Chiron, it's essential to address any emotional blocks or limiting beliefs around money to create a healthier relationship with your finances.

Evaluate your spending habits and financial goals. Create a realistic budget that allows you to meet your needs while also saving for the future. Consider seeking advice from a financial professional to ensure you are making sound financial decisions.

This is also a favorable time to explore new sources of income or investment opportunities. However, exercise caution and do thorough research before committing to any financial ventures. Seek guidance from experts if necessary, as they can provide valuable insights and help you make informed decisions.

Maintain a balanced approach to money. Avoid impulsive purchases or risky investments that could potentially strain your financial stability. Focus on long-term financial security and establish healthy saving habits. By cultivating a mindset of abundance and financial responsibility, you can create a solid foundation for your future.

Remember to enjoy the present moment and not let financial worries overshadow your overall well-being. Find joy in simple pleasures and practice gratitude for the abundance that already exists in your life. By adopting a positive mindset, you can attract prosperity and financial abundance.

Health

In July, Cancer individuals are encouraged to prioritize their health and well-being. With the Sun's square to Chiron, there may be opportunities for emotional healing and physical rejuvenation.

Pay attention to your emotional health and seek ways to release any pent-up emotions or stress. Engage in activities that promote emotional well-being, such as meditation, journaling, or therapy. Nurture your relationships and surround yourself with a supportive network of friends and family.

Physical health is also important during this period. Establish a consistent exercise routine that suits your preferences and energy levels. Engage in activities that bring you joy, whether it's yoga, swimming, or hiking. Prioritize nutritious meals and stay hydrated to support your overall well-being.

Be mindful of your energy levels and avoid overexerting yourself. Find a balance between work, rest, and play. Practice self-care rituals that help you relax and recharge, such as taking warm baths, reading, or spending time in nature. Listen to your body's signals and honor its need for rest and rejuvenation.

Regular check-ups with healthcare professionals are crucial to monitor your health and address any concerns. Don't hesitate to seek medical advice or support if needed. Prevention is key, so take proactive measures to maintain your health and well-being.

Remember that emotional and physical health are interconnected. By nurturing your emotional well-being and taking care of your physical body, you can achieve a harmonious balance that supports your overall health and happiness.

Travel

Travel opportunities arise for Cancer individuals in July, offering a chance to explore new horizons and expand their perspectives. With Mars' trine to Pluto, there is a sense of adventure and transformation associated with your journeys.

When planning your travels, consider destinations that offer a mix of natural beauty and cultural experiences. Seek out places where you can connect with nature, such as serene beaches, majestic mountains, or lush forests. Immersing yourself in the healing power of nature can provide a sense of peace and rejuvenation.

Cultural exploration can also be enriching during this period. Visit historical sites, museums, or engage in local traditions and customs. Embrace the opportunity to learn about different cultures and broaden your understanding of the world.

Maintain a balance between exploration and relaxation during your travels. Allow yourself time for rest and rejuvenation, as excessive travel can sometimes drain your energy. Engage in self-care practices such as meditation, yoga, or spa treatments to maintain a sense of balance and well-being.

Whether you're traveling alone or with loved ones, embrace the spirit of adventure and remain open to new experiences. Connect with locals, try new cuisines, and step out of your comfort zone. Travel is not only about the destination but also about the inner transformation and personal growth it can bring.

Ensure that you take necessary safety precautions while traveling. Research your destinations, be aware of local customs and laws, and prioritize your well-being at all times. Travel insurance and proper documentation are essential to ensure a smooth and hassle-free journey.

Embrace the joy of exploration and allow your travels to expand your horizons, both internally and externally. Each journey has the potential to create lasting memories and shape your perspective on life.

Insight from the stars

"Embrace the ebb and flow of life, for within the waves lie hidden treasures of growth and transformation." - The stars encourage Cancer individuals to embrace the natural cycles of life, understanding that both joys and challenges bring opportunities for personal evolution.

Best days of the month: July 2nd, 9th, 13th, 18th, 22nd, 30th, and 31st.

August 2024

Horoscope

In August, Cancer individuals can expect a dynamic and transformative period in various aspects of life. The astrological influences urge you to embrace change, release old patterns, and step into a renewed sense of self.

The month begins with Mars sextile the True Node, indicating a harmonious alignment of your actions and life path. You have a strong sense of purpose and are motivated to make positive changes in your life. Use this energy to pursue your goals and align your actions with your long-term aspirations.

Venus squares Uranus on August 2, bringing potential disruptions or surprises in your relationships and finances. It's essential to remain adaptable and open-minded during this time. Embrace unexpected changes and find creative solutions to challenges that arise.

The Sun's biquintile with Saturn on August 4 provides an opportunity to find a balance between your individuality and responsibilities. You may feel a strong desire for stability and structure in your life. Use this energy to establish healthy routines and prioritize your long-term goals.

Mars quintile Neptune on August 6 enhances your intuition and spiritual connection. Trust your instincts and listen to the subtle guidance of your inner voice. This energy supports creative and imaginative pursuits, allowing you to channel your emotions into artistic expression.

Mercury's conjunction with Venus on August 7 enhances communication and relationships. This alignment promotes harmony and understanding in your interactions with others. It's an excellent time for heartfelt conversations and expressing your feelings with clarity and compassion.

The Sun's quincunx with Saturn on August 10 may bring some temporary challenges or frustrations in your professional or personal life. Remain patient and adaptable, and seek practical solutions to overcome obstacles.

Venus's quincunx with True Node on August 11
and sesquiquadrate with Chiron on August 11 highlight
the importance of balancing your personal needs with
the needs of your relationships. Find a middle ground
where you can express yourself authentically while
also considering the well-being of others.

The month continues with various planetary aspects
that encourage self-expression, communication, and
self-reflection. The Sun's sesquiquadrate with True
Node on August 14 and trine with Chiron on August
15 invite you to embrace your individuality and share
your unique gifts with the world.

Embrace the transformative energy and use it to
align your actions with your long-term goals and
aspirations.

Love

In matters of love, August brings a mix of energies
for Cancer individuals. Venus's square with Uranus on
August 2 may introduce some unexpected changes or
disruptions in your relationships. This can create
excitement and novelty but also challenges in finding
stability and balance. Be open to new experiences and
be willing to adapt to unexpected shifts in your
romantic life.

The Sun's biquintile with Saturn on August 4 encourages you to find a healthy balance between personal freedom and commitment in your relationships. It's a time to establish boundaries and prioritize your own needs while also nurturing your partnerships. Seek stability and structure in your love life while allowing room for growth and individuality.

Venus's quincunx with Neptune on August 4 and quincunx with Pluto on August 5 call for clarity and discernment in matters of the heart. Be aware of potential illusions or unrealistic expectations in relationships. Take time to reassess your values, needs, and desires to ensure that you are in alignment with your authentic self. Avoid being overly influenced by external factors or societal pressures.

Mars quintile Neptune on August 6 enhances your intuitive and spiritual connection, allowing you to tap into the deeper emotional realms of your relationships. Trust your instincts and listen to the subtle messages from your heart. This energy supports romantic gestures, creative expressions of love, and deepening emotional connections.

Venus's sesquiquadrate with Chiron on August 11 highlights the importance of healing and addressing any past wounds or insecurities that may affect your relationships. It's an opportunity for emotional growth and self-reflection, as you work through any relationship patterns or fears that may hinder your ability to fully embrace love.

The Sun's trine with Chiron on August 15 fosters a sense of emotional healing and empathy in your relationships. This is a favorable time for open and honest communication, where you can express your vulnerabilities and offer support to your partner. Deep connections and emotional intimacy are highlighted during this period.

Venus's trine with Uranus on August 27 brings excitement and a desire for freedom in your romantic life. You may be drawn to unconventional relationships or experiences that offer novelty and adventure. Embrace spontaneity and explore new ways of connecting with your partner or meeting new potential love interests.

Career

With the Sun's biquintile with Saturn on August 4, you are encouraged to find a balance between structure and innovation in your work. This is a favorable time to establish solid foundations, set realistic goals, and implement long-term plans. Focus on building a strong professional reputation and maintaining a disciplined work ethic.

Mercury's biquintile with Neptune on August 23 enhances your imagination and intuition, allowing you to tap into your creative potential and find innovative solutions to challenges in the workplace. Trust your instincts and don't be afraid to think outside the box. Your ability to communicate and express your ideas in a captivating manner can lead to positive collaborations and successful projects.

Venus's trine with Jupiter on August 14 brings favorable energy for networking, collaborations, and expanding your professional circle. This is a great time to attend social events, engage in team projects, or seek out mentorship opportunities. Your positive and optimistic attitude will attract support and opportunities for growth.

Mars's conjunction with Jupiter on August 14 ignites your ambition and drive to excel in your career. You may feel a surge of confidence and enthusiasm, inspiring you to take on new challenges and pursue your professional goals with determination. This alignment favors leadership roles, public speaking, and ventures that require assertiveness and initiative.

The Sun's trine with Chiron on August 15 highlights the importance of self-care and emotional well-being in the workplace. Take time to nurture yourself and create a healthy work-life balance. This will enhance your productivity, creativity, and overall job satisfaction. Seek opportunities for personal growth and professional development that align with your passions and values.

Venus's trine with Uranus on August 27 brings unexpected opportunities and breakthroughs in your career. Be open to innovative ideas, embrace change, and be willing to take calculated risks. This energy supports entrepreneurial endeavors, unique projects, and collaborations that bring a fresh and exciting perspective to your professional life.

Finance

The Sun's quincunx with Saturn on August 10 reminds you to be disciplined and responsible when it comes to financial matters. Take a critical look at your spending habits and assess where you can make adjustments. This is a favorable time to create a practical budget and stick to it, ensuring that your expenses are aligned with your financial goals.

Venus's opposition with Neptune on August 28 cautions against impulsive or overly idealistic financial decisions. Be wary of get-rich-quick schemes or investments that seem too good to be true. It's important to do thorough research and seek professional advice before making any major financial commitments. Trust your instincts and be discerning with your choices.

The Venus-Pluto trine on August 29 brings the potential for financial transformation and empowerment. This is a favorable time to review your financial strategies and consider long-term investments that can provide stability and growth. Engage in financial planning, consult with experts, and explore opportunities for wealth accumulation and security.

Mercury's sesquiquadrate with True Node on August 31 suggests the need for careful assessment of your financial goals and the alignment of your actions with your true values. Evaluate whether your financial pursuits are in line with your authentic self and make adjustments as necessary. This alignment encourages you to prioritize financial endeavors that contribute to your personal growth and fulfillment.

It's also crucial to maintain a balanced approach to your finances, allowing room for both practicality and enjoyment. Treat yourself within reason, but also ensure that you are saving and investing wisely for the future. Seek ways to increase your financial literacy and explore avenues for additional income or career advancement.

Remember to cultivate an attitude of gratitude and abundance, appreciating the resources you have while also striving for financial stability. With careful planning, a discerning eye, and a commitment to your long-term financial goals, you can navigate the

financial landscape in August with confidence and
resilience.

Health

The Sun's sesquiquadrate with Chiron on August 6
calls for attention to any emotional wounds or
unresolved issues that may be affecting your overall
well-being. Take time to reflect on your emotional
state and engage in healing practices such as therapy,
meditation, or journaling. Nurturing your emotional
health is essential for maintaining a strong foundation
for your physical well-being.

The Mars-Jupiter conjunction on August 14 brings
a boost of energy and motivation. Use this opportunity
to engage in physical activities that bring you joy and
help you stay fit. Incorporate regular exercise routines
into your daily life, whether it's through outdoor
activities, gym workouts, or group classes. Movement
and physical exertion will not only benefit your
physical health but also contribute to your mental and
emotional well-being.

Venus's trine with Uranus on August 27 encourages
you to explore new ways to care for your body and
enhance your overall vitality. Consider incorporating
alternative therapies or holistic practices into your
wellness routine. This could include acupuncture,

yoga, herbal remedies, or energy healing modalities. Embrace a holistic approach to health that nurtures both your body and spirit.

Mercury's sesquiquadrate with True Node on August 31 reminds you to pay attention to the mind-body connection. Mental well-being plays a significant role in physical health, so make an effort to cultivate positive thoughts and manage stress effectively. Incorporate stress-reduction techniques into your daily routine, such as mindfulness meditation, deep breathing exercises, or engaging in hobbies and activities that bring you joy.

Remember to prioritize rest and rejuvenation. Schedule regular downtime and ensure you're getting sufficient sleep each night. Establish a consistent sleep routine and create a peaceful sleep environment that supports deep, restorative rest.

Maintaining a balanced diet is also crucial for your overall health. Focus on consuming whole, nutrient-dense foods and staying hydrated. Pay attention to any dietary sensitivities or allergies that may impact your well-being.

Travel

With the Sun's trine to Uranus on August 4, you may feel an urge for spontaneity and a willingness to step out of your comfort zone. This aspect encourages you to embrace unique travel experiences and seek out destinations that offer a sense of adventure and novelty. Consider visiting off-the-beaten-path locations or participating in activities that allow you to connect with the local culture and traditions.

The Venus-Mars square on August 22 may bring some challenges or delays in travel plans. It is advisable to remain flexible and patient during this time. If unexpected obstacles arise, approach them with a calm and adaptable mindset. Use this opportunity to practice patience and resilience, knowing that delays or changes in plans can lead to new and unexpected experiences.

August 28 brings Venus's opposition to Neptune, which inspires a desire for relaxation and rejuvenation. This aspect encourages you to seek out destinations that offer tranquility and a connection to nature. Consider retreats, spa getaways, or destinations known for their natural beauty. Engaging in activities such as hiking, beachcombing, or nature walks can help you find peace and rejuvenation.

Mercury's sesquiquadrate with the True Node on August 31 may bring some communication challenges during your travels. It is important to remain mindful of your words and to be patient and understanding in your interactions with others. Keep an open mind and embrace opportunities for cultural exchange and learning.

Insights from the stars

August 2024 is a period of transition for Cancer. It's a time to reflect, reorganize, and reassess various aspects of life, including relationships, career, and finances. While there may be moments of doubt and uncertainty, remember that these are temporary. Stay patient, take things in stride, and look forward to the favorable changes coming your way.

Best days of the month: August 2nd, 10th, 15th, 19th, 22nd, and 31st .

September 2024

Horoscope

In September, Cancer, you'll experience a blend of emotional depth and practicality, urging you to find a balance between your inner world and outer responsibilities. The month begins with Mercury forming a trine with Chiron on September 2nd, fostering healing conversations and self-reflection. This aspect encourages you to express your emotions and address any emotional wounds that may hinder your personal growth.

On September 6th, the Sun squares Jupiter, presenting opportunities for expansion, but also a need to maintain a grounded perspective. It's crucial to strike a balance between optimism and practicality, ensuring that you don't become overwhelmed by lofty goals or unrealistic expectations.

Mercury squares Uranus on September 7th, enhancing your communication skills but also causing a potential clash between your desire for independence and the need for collaboration. Find a middle ground that allows you to express your unique ideas while remaining open to the perspectives of others.

The mid-month period brings significant astrological events that impact your relationships and self-expression. On September 12th, the Sun opposes Saturn, challenging your sense of self and urging you to confront any self-imposed limitations. This is an opportunity for growth and self-discovery, as you redefine your identity and embrace your personal power.

Mars's square with Neptune on September 13th may create confusion or a sense of disillusionment in your professional life. It's important to trust your instincts and be cautious of potential deception or misleading information. Take your time before making important decisions or commitments.

As the month progresses, the emphasis shifts towards partnerships and collaborations. Venus trines Jupiter on September 15th, fostering harmonious connections and bringing joy to your relationships. This is an excellent time for social gatherings, romantic encounters, and cooperative endeavors. Embrace the opportunities for growth and expansion in your personal connections.

The Sun's opposition to Neptune on September 20th
may bring a temporary sense of uncertainty or
confusion. Take time for introspection and self-
reflection, as this aspect urges you to reassess your
goals and align them with your true passions and
aspirations. Trust your intuition and let go of any
illusions that may be hindering your progress.

Love

In matters of the heart, September encourages
Cancer to embrace vulnerability and open themselves
up to deeper emotional connections. Venus opposes the
True Node on September 3rd, potentially bringing
romantic encounters or relationship challenges that
require careful navigation. This aspect prompts you to
assess whether certain relationships align with your
long-term goals and personal growth.

Mid-month, Venus trines Jupiter, creating a
harmonious and expansive atmosphere for love.
Existing relationships may deepen, and single Cancers
may attract potential partners who align with their
values and aspirations. It's an ideal time to express your
affections, nurture the bonds you cherish, and explore
new possibilities for emotional connection.

Career

Career-wise, September presents promising prospects for Cancer individuals. The opposition between the Sun and Saturn on September 8th may initially challenge your sense of authority and require you to confront obstacles. However, this serves as an opportunity for growth, perseverance, and demonstrating your resilience in the face of adversity.

As a Cancer, your natural intuition and nurturing qualities will be particularly valuable in the workplace this month. Trust your instincts when making decisions and rely on your ability to create harmonious working environments. Your empathetic nature will make you a sought-after team member, and your ability to understand the needs and emotions of others will be instrumental in resolving conflicts and fostering cooperation.

Finance

September brings stability and opportunities for financial growth for Cancer individuals. The harmonious trine between Venus and Jupiter on September 15th signals positive financial prospects and the potential for financial gains through partnerships or joint ventures.

This is an ideal time to focus on long-term financial planning and investments. However, exercise caution and ensure you thoroughly research any investment opportunities before committing. Seek the guidance of a financial advisor if needed.

Health

In terms of health, September encourages Cancer individuals to prioritize self-care and emotional well-being. The opposition between the Sun and Neptune on September 20th may bring moments of emotional sensitivity and a need for relaxation and self-reflection.

Pay attention to your emotional needs and engage in activities that promote relaxation and stress reduction. Engaging in meditation, yoga, or other mindfulness practices can provide immense benefits for your overall well-being. Taking time for self-care and nurturing your emotional health will have a positive impact on your physical health as well.

Travel

September offers opportunities for meaningful travel experiences that enrich your perspective and expand your horizons. Planetary aspects do not indicate any significant challenges or disruptions during this month, providing a favorable environment for exploring new destinations, immersing yourself in different cultures, or embarking on spiritual retreats. Embrace the transformative power of travel and allow yourself to be inspired by the world around you.

Insights from the stars

Dear Cancer, embrace the changes that September brings and use them as opportunities for growth. Ground yourself with the earthy Virgo energy and set practical goals for different aspects of your life.

Best days of the month: September 3rd, 8th, 15th, 16th, 20th, 22nd, and 26th.

October 2024

Horoscope

In October, Cancer, you will experience a profound and transformative energy that will deeply influence various areas of your life. This month holds a potent mix of cosmic alignments that invite you to embark on a journey of self-discovery, personal transformation, and courageous action.

The celestial energies encourage you to delve into the depths of your emotions and explore your inner world. It is a time of introspection and self-reflection, where you have the opportunity to uncover hidden aspects of your psyche and heal emotional wounds. This inner work will pave the way for personal growth and a greater understanding of yourself and your desires.

The trine between Mercury and Saturn on October 22nd enhances your communication skills and intellectual prowess. It is an excellent time to engage in important negotiations, present your ideas with conviction, and establish solid professional connections. Your ability to articulate your thoughts clearly and concisely will leave a positive impression on others, potentially opening doors for career advancements or new opportunities.

In conclusion, October holds transformative energies that invite you to embark on a journey of self-discovery, personal growth, and courageous action. By embracing the depths of your emotions, nurturing your relationships, and prioritizing self-care, you can navigate this month with grace and emerge stronger and wiser. Remember to balance your financial decisions, seize professional opportunities, and embrace the adventures that await you on your path of personal evolution.

Love

For Cancerians in relationships, October presents a period of emotional intensity and potential for profound connection. The trine between Venus and Mars on October 8th ignites passion and harmonizes the energies between you and your partner. It's a time of increased romance, intimacy, and a deepening bond.

However, the square between Venus and Saturn on October 28th may introduce challenges that require patience and understanding. It's crucial to communicate openly, listen empathetically, and work together to find compromises. This period can lead to a stronger and more resilient partnership if approached with compassion and willingness to grow together.

For single Cancerians, October brings the potential for unexpected encounters and romantic opportunities. The opposition between Venus and Uranus on October 14th may spark intense attraction or lead to a connection with someone who challenges your comfort zone. Embrace these experiences as catalysts for personal growth and exploration of new possibilities.

Career

In your professional life, October holds great potential for growth and advancement. The Sun's opposition to Chiron on October 13th calls for self-reflection and addressing any insecurities that may hinder your progress. By acknowledging and working through these barriers, you pave the way for increased confidence and professional breakthroughs.

The trine between Mercury and Saturn on October 22nd enhances your communication skills and mental acuity. It's an excellent time to present your ideas, engage in negotiations, and establish strong professional relationships. Your ability to articulate your thoughts and demonstrate your expertise will be highly influential in achieving your career goals.

Finance

Financially, October presents a mixed landscape that requires cautious decision-making. The trine between Venus and Saturn on October 4th supports financial stability, wise investments, and long-term planning. It's an opportune time to evaluate your financial goals, create a budget, and make strategic choices that align with your future aspirations.

However, the square between Venus and Jupiter on October 10th warns against impulsive spending and overindulgence. Be mindful of your financial choices, resist the temptation of immediate gratification, and prioritize long-term financial security. Exercise discipline and seek a balance between enjoying life's pleasures and maintaining fiscal responsibility.

Health

Your well-being and self-care take center stage in October, Cancer. The Sun's quincunx aspect with Uranus on October 19th serves as a reminder to maintain balance and avoid overexertion. Nurture your physical, mental, and emotional health by incorporating self-care practices into your daily routine.

Listen to your body's signals and make adjustments as needed. Prioritize stress-management techniques, engage in regular exercise, and nourish yourself with wholesome foods. Creating a harmonious balance between work and rest is vital for maintaining your overall well-being.

Travel

October offers favorable energies for travel and exploration. The biquintile aspect between Mercury and Jupiter on October 23rd sparks your sense of adventure and curiosity. Whether it's a spontaneous day trip or a carefully planned vacation, embrace the opportunity to expand your horizons and immerse yourself in new experiences.

Be open to discovering different cultures, trying new cuisines, and engaging with unfamiliar environments. Travel not only broadens your perspective but also provides valuable opportunities for personal growth and self-discovery.

Insight from the stars

"Embrace the discomfort of growth, for it is the soil in which your dreams flourish. Trust the process and allow yourself to transform."

Best days of the month: October 8th, 13th, 14th, 22nd, 28th and 31st.

November 2024

Horoscope

Dear Cancer, November 2024 promises to be a transformative and dynamic month for you. The planetary aspects indicate a blend of intense energies and harmonious influences that will shape various areas of your life. It is a time of self-discovery, healing, and growth.

The sextile between Jupiter and Chiron on November 2nd sets the tone for the month by emphasizing personal healing and spiritual growth. This aspect encourages you to delve into your past wounds and explore deeper aspects of your psyche. By embracing vulnerability and learning from your past experiences, you can move forward with greater wisdom and understanding.

On the same day, the trine between Mercury and Mars enhances your communication skills and mental agility. Your ability to express yourself effectively will be heightened, making it an excellent time for important conversations, negotiations, or intellectual pursuits. This aspect also boosts your energy and motivation, allowing you to take decisive action towards your goals.

The sextile between Mercury and Pluto on November 2nd further amplifies your mental prowess. It grants you the ability to delve deep into complex subjects and uncover hidden truths. This aspect supports research, investigation, and uncovering profound insights. It is a favorable time for introspection and personal growth.

However, the opposition between Mars and Pluto on November 3rd brings a potential for power struggles and conflicts. You may encounter resistance or opposition from others during this time. It is crucial to handle these situations with tact and diplomacy, avoiding confrontations whenever possible. This aspect also signals a need to examine and transform any deep-seated emotional patterns or hidden desires that may be holding you back.

The opposition between Venus and Jupiter on November 3rd highlights relationships and social interactions. It may intensify your desires for pleasure and romance. However, it is essential to avoid excessive indulgence or unrealistic expectations. Use this time to strengthen existing connections and explore new possibilities with an open heart and mind. Balance your desires with a practical outlook to avoid disappointment.

Love

In matters of the heart, November 2024 offers opportunities for deep emotional connections and relationship growth. The opposition between Venus and Jupiter on November 3rd may intensify your desires for pleasure and romance. However, it is important to approach relationships with caution and temper your expectations. Avoid the pitfalls of excessive indulgence and idealistic fantasies. Focus on building meaningful connections based on trust, understanding, and open communication. For those who are single, this period brings the potential for new and exciting romantic possibilities. Take your time to truly get to know potential partners and allow relationships to develop organically.

Career

Cancer, November 2024 presents opportunities for growth and advancement in your career. The trine between the Sun and Saturn on November 4th brings stability and support. Your hard work and dedication will be recognized, potentially leading to professional advancements and increased responsibilities. This aspect urges you to set long-term goals and make practical plans for your future. Take advantage of the positive energy to lay solid foundations for your career success. Seek guidance from mentors or superiors, as their advice can provide valuable insights and help you navigate your professional path.

Finance

Financially, November 2024 calls for caution and strategic planning. The square between Venus and Neptune on November 9th may introduce confusion or uncertainty into your financial matters. It is crucial to exercise prudence and avoid impulsive decisions or risky investments. Take the time to review your financial situation, create a budget, and seek professional advice if needed. Stay focused on your long-term financial goals and resist the temptation of get-rich-quick schemes. Consider diversifying your income sources and explore practical ways to save and invest wisely. With careful planning and disciplined financial management, you can maintain stability and work towards long-term prosperity.

Health

Cancer, your well-being takes precedence in
November 2024. The sesquiquadrate between the Sun
and Neptune on November 4th emphasizes the need for
rest and self-care. Pay attention to both your physical
and emotional health, as this aspect may make you
more susceptible to stress or fatigue. Incorporate
relaxation techniques, such as meditation or yoga, into
your daily routine to find inner balance. Engage in
regular exercise to maintain vitality and boost your
immune system. Nourish your body with a healthy diet,
ensuring you get enough restorative sleep. Listen to
your body's needs and seek support if you're feeling
overwhelmed or experiencing emotional challenges.
Prioritize self-care to maintain overall well-being.

Travel

November 2024 presents opportunities for exciting
and enriching travel experiences for Cancerians. The
biquintile between Venus and Uranus on November
12th ignites a sense of adventure and spontaneity. This
aspect encourages you to explore new horizons and
embrace unique experiences. Consider planning a short
getaway to a new destination or engaging in activities

that broaden your horizons. Travel provides an opportunity to step out of your comfort zone and gain fresh insights and inspiration. Whether you embark on a solo trip or travel with loved ones, embrace the spirit of adventure and let the world ignite your curiosity. Be open to the unexpected, as these experiences can broaden your perspective and enrich your life.

Insight from the stars

The advice from the stars for November 2024 is to not take everything literally. By doing this, you'll be pleasantly surprised at the seriousness and constancy of some people towards you.

Best days of the month: November 2nd, 4th, 12th, 18th, 23rd, 27th, and 29th.

December 2024

Horoscope

In December 2024, Cancer, the planetary movements bring significant shifts and opportunities in various aspects of your life. As the year comes to a close, it's a time of reflection and preparation for the new year ahead. The aspects during this month encourage you to focus on personal growth, nurturing relationships, and creating a solid foundation for the future.

The month begins with a Venus biquintile Jupiter aspect on December 1st, fostering a harmonious energy that promotes love, abundance, and expansion. This aspect enhances your ability to attract positivity and deepen connections with loved ones. It's an ideal time to strengthen your bonds and express your affections openly.

Mercury's trine to Chiron on December 2nd encourages healing conversations and self-reflection. This aspect supports you in addressing emotional wounds and finding resolutions in relationships. Use this time to engage in meaningful dialogue and express your needs and concerns with compassion.

In the realm of career, the square between the Sun and Saturn on December 4th may bring challenges and responsibilities. It's important to stay focused and determined, even in the face of obstacles. This aspect calls for discipline and perseverance as you work towards your professional goals. Use this time to demonstrate your capabilities and prove your worth.

When it comes to finances, the Venus trine Uranus aspect on December 2nd brings a touch of excitement and unexpected opportunities. Keep an open mind and be receptive to new ideas or investments that may come your way. However, exercise caution and conduct thorough research before making any significant financial decisions.

Love

Love takes center stage for Cancerians in December 2024. The Venus opposition Mars aspect on December 12th ignites passion and intensity in your romantic relationships. This aspect may bring moments of conflict or power struggles, but it also provides an opportunity for growth and deeper understanding. It's essential to approach any challenges with open communication, empathy, and a willingness to compromise.

For those seeking love, the Venus sextile Jupiter aspect on December 2nd creates an atmosphere of optimism and abundance. This aspect enhances your charisma and attractiveness, making you more likely to attract potential partners. Embrace social opportunities and be open to new connections. However, remember to take things slow and ensure that you truly align with the values and aspirations of your potential love interests.

Career

Career-wise, December 2024 offers both challenges and opportunities for Cancerians. The Sun square Saturn aspect on December 4th may bring a sense of pressure and responsibility in your professional life. It's crucial to stay focused, organized, and disciplined during this time. Embrace your tasks with determination and prioritize long-term goals. This aspect tests your perseverance and resilience, allowing you to demonstrate your capabilities and commitment.

Additionally, the Sun biquintile Mars aspect on December 20th ignites your drive and ambition. Use this energy to take decisive action, assert yourself, and pursue your career aspirations. Trust your instincts and have confidence in your abilities. This aspect provides a boost of motivation and may bring opportunities for advancement or recognition.

Finance

December 2024 brings a mix of stability and unexpected financial opportunities for Cancerians. The Venus trine Uranus aspect on December 2nd may introduce unique avenues for increasing your income. Stay open to new ideas or investments that come your way, but be cautious and conduct thorough research before committing to any financial ventures.

The Venus sextile Neptune aspect on December 4th encourages you to find a balance between practicality and generosity in your financial dealings. It's important to prioritize your financial well-being while also considering the needs of others. This aspect promotes acts of kindness and may inspire you to give back or contribute to charitable causes.

Remember to maintain a budget and exercise responsible financial management throughout the month. By staying mindful of your spending habits and prioritizing your financial goals, you can make the most of the opportunities that arise and build a stable foundation for your future.

Health

In terms of health, December 2024 encourages Cancerians to prioritize self-care and well-being. The Mercury square Saturn aspect on December 6th may bring some mental or emotional challenges. It's essential to manage stress levels and practice self-care routines that support your overall health and vitality.

Take time to relax, engage in activities that bring you joy, and maintain a balanced lifestyle. Consider incorporating meditation, yoga, or other mindfulness practices into your daily routine to cultivate inner peace and mental clarity.

Pay attention to your physical health as well. With the Sun square Neptune aspect on December 18th, it's important to ensure you're getting enough rest and practicing healthy habits. Take care of your immune system by nourishing your body with nutritious foods and staying hydrated.

If you're feeling overwhelmed or experiencing any health concerns, don't hesitate to seek support from healthcare professionals. Remember, taking care of your well-being is essential for maintaining balance and enjoying the festive season.

Travel

December 2024 presents exciting opportunities for travel and exploration for Cancerians. The Sun biquintile Uranus aspect on December 21st sparks a sense of adventure and a desire for new experiences. Consider planning a spontaneous trip or embarking on an adventure that expands your horizons. Whether it's a short getaway or a more extended vacation, travel can provide valuable opportunities for personal growth and rejuvenation.

When traveling, remember to prioritize safety and be prepared for any unexpected circumstances. Take necessary precautions, research your destinations, and have contingency plans in place. Embrace the spirit of adventure while also ensuring your well-being.

Traveling with loved ones can deepen your connections and create lasting memories. Consider planning trips or activities that allow you to bond and strengthen your relationships. Whether it's a romantic getaway or a family vacation, shared experiences can foster deeper connections and create cherished moments.

Insight from the stars

The stars in December 2024 whisper of a turning point for Cancer. This is a month of endings and beginnings. Embrace the transformations with grace and gratitude. There's a strong cosmic push towards self-improvement and personal growth. The choices you make this month will resonate through the coming year. Trust your intuition and be the master of your destiny.

Best days of the month: December 2nd, 10th, 13th, 19th, 20th, 24th and 31st.

Printed in Great Britain
by Amazon